A to Z

United States of America

BY JEFF REYNOLDS

children's press®
A Division of Scholastic Inc.
New York Toronto London Auckland Sydney
Mexico City New Delhi Hong Kong
Danbury, Connecticut

WITHDRAWN
PARK FOREST PUBLIC LIBRARY 60466

Series Consultant: Jeanne Nicholson Siler
Series Design: Marie O'Neill
Photo Research: Candlepants Incorporated

For my parents, Jim and Eunice Reynolds — J.R.

The photos on the cover show a bald eagle (top left), Mount Rushmore (top right), lobster (bottom right), and American children (bottom left).

Photographs © 2004: Animals Animals/Earth Scenes: 5 top right (Richard Kettlewell), cover top (McDonald Wildlife Photography); AP/Wide World Photos: 33 top right (Gene Herrick), 11 left, 33 bottom; Art Resource, NY/National Portrait Gallery, Smithsonian Institution, Washington DC: 15 top right; Corbis Images: 4, 5 top left (Theo Allofs), 37 bottom left (Morton Beebe), 13, 15 bottom left, 15 top left, 23 bottom (Bettmann), 6 right (D. Boone), 5 bottom left (Tom Brakefield), 28 (Duomo), 17 left (Ric Ergenbright), 29 top (Najlah Feanny), 10 top (Sandy Felsenthal), 5 bottom right (Mitchell Gerber), 39 (Philip Gould), 9 top right (Robert Holmes), 32 (Hulton-Deutsch Collection), 6 left (Douglas Mesney), 12 right (Museum of the City of New York), 10 bottom (Lance Nelson), 16 bottom (Richard T. Nowitz), 30 (Owaki - Kulla), 34 top (Reuters), cover center left, 27 (Royalty-Free), 35 bottom (Phil Schermeister), 33 top left (Flip Schulke), 8 left (Paul A. Souders), 35 top left (Jim Sugar), 26 (Ron Watts), 5 bottom right (Jim Zuckerman), 14; David Sanger Photography: 25 bottom; Getty Images: cover bottom (Davies + Starr), 24 center (David Young-Wolff); Index Stock Imagery: 37 right (Tim Brown), 37 top left (David Loveall), 36 (Wendell Metzen); Library of Congress: 12 left (via SODA), 23 top; Mark Downey/Lucid Images: 24 top; Michael Sewell/Visual Pursuit: 24 bottom; National Archives and Records Administration: 22 top; National Geographic Image Collection/Panoramic Images/Warren Marr: 18, 19; PhotoDisc/Getty Images: cover center right (Don Farall), 8 right (Siede Preis), 11 right; PictureHistory.com: 22 bottom; Stone/Getty Images: 35 top right (David Hiser), 34 bottom (Rohan); Taxi/Getty Images: 25 top (Jim Bastardo), 16 top (Bryan Peterson), 17 right (Mark Scott), 28 top (Arthur Tilley); The Image Bank/Getty Images/Michael Setboun: 7; The Image Works: 9 top right (Jeff Greenberg), 9 bottom (David Grossman), 29 bottom (Science Museum, London/Topham-HIP), 31 (Teake Zuidema).
Map by XNR Productions

Library of Congress Cataloging-in-Publication Data

Reynolds, Jeff E., 1958-
  United States of America / by Jeff Reynolds.
    p. cm. — (A to Z)
  Includes bibliographical references and index.
Contents: Animals - Buildings - Cities - Dress - Exports - Food - Government - History - Important people - Jobs - Keepsakes - Land - Map - Nation - Only in USA - People - Question - Religion - School and sports - Transportation - Unusual Places - Visiting the Country - Window to the past - X-tra special things - Yearly Festivals - Zydeco - Let's Explore More.
  ISBN 0-516-23659-8 (lib. bdg.)   0-516-25074-4 (pbk.)
  1. United States—Juvenile literature. I. Title. II. Series.
  E156.R49 2004
  973—dc22
                                2004009118

©2004 by Scholastic Inc.
All rights reserved. Published simultaneously in Canada.
Printed in the United States of America.
CHILDREN'S PRESS and associated logos are trademarks and or registered trademarks of Scholastic Library Publishing. SCHOLASTIC and associated logos are trademarks and or registered trademarks of Scholastic Inc.

1 2 3 4 5 6 7 8 9 10 R 13 12 11 10 09 08 07 06 05 04

 Contents

OCT 1 8 2004

Animals

The bald eagle is a symbol of the United States.

The bald eagle, wild turkey, bison, and grizzly bear are just a few of the amazing animals that live in the United States of America.

In the 1800's, bison were hunted until there were only 1,000 of them left.

Some thought the wild turkey was a better symbol of the United States.

Why was the bald eagle chosen as the symbol of the United States? Americans wanted their symbol to be different from other nations. They chose the bald eagle because it is a kind of eagle found only in North America.

Bison are also great animals. Bison are also called buffalo. People worked hard to stop hunters from killing bison. Now there are thousands of bison.

Look at the teeth on that grizzly bear! Grizzlies were once found in many parts of the country. Today, in the United States, grizzlies live only in Alaska and in some of the states of the Northwest.

The grizzly bear is the largest land predator in the world.

The Alamo was originally a Spanish mission, or religious settlement.

The Space Needle stands tall among Seattle's skyscrapers.

Buildings

The world's first skyscrapers were built in the United States. Some skyscrapers, such as the Empire State Building in New York City and the Space Needle in Seattle, Washington, are important American **landmarks**.

Many old buildings in the United States are landmarks, too. They are protected because of their importance to American history. One of these is the Alamo in San Antonio, Texas. The Alamo is the **site** of a famous battle Texans fought during their war for independence from Mexico.

The Brooklyn Bridge is a famous landmark in New York City.

Cities

New York City is the most populated city in the United States. It is also one of the largest cities in the world. More than eight million people live there. New York City is divided into five sections. They are called **boroughs**. They are Manhattan, Queens, Brooklyn, Statan Island, and the Bronx.

Los Angeles, California, has only about half as many people as New York City. It is the United States' second-largest city. Chicago, Illinois, is third. Its population is just under three million. Houston, Texas, and Philadelphia, Pennsylvania, are other cities with large populations.

Dress

Early settlers in America brought clothes with them from Europe.

Native American girls perform a traditional dance in ceremonial clothing.

Cowboy boots are one item of clothing that everyone associates with the United States.

Amish people have strict rules about the clothing they wear.

The Pilgrim settlers of Massachusetts dressed much like they did back in England.

Today, most Americans dress for work and play in casual, comfortable clothes.

Buckskin clothing was worn by Native Americans and by European settlers in wilderness areas. It was made from deerskin. Fur and leather from other animals was also used. Farmers kept flocks of sheep and used their wool to make cloth. Eventually, southern farmers began to grow cotton. It became the material used for many clothes.

Today, the United States is home to a large fashion **industry**. Clothing designed and made in the United States is worn by people around the world.

Canada buys most of the cars exported by the United States.

Exports

The United States is the world's leading exporter of corn.

Cars, airplanes, and computers are some of America's main exports, but food is also important. The United States grows more of some foods than it needs. Extra grain and meat are exported to countries like Japan, where farms are small.

American culture is an important export, too. American music and films are enjoyed by people in many parts of the world.

Peanut Butter Sandwich Recipe

WHAT YOU NEED:
- 2 slices of bread
- 2 tablespoons peanut butter
- your choice of other ingredients

HOW TO MAKE IT:
Spread peanut butter evenly over one slice of bread. Add your favorite ingredients on top. Use grape jelly, raisins, or slices of banana for a sweet taste. Lettuce, slices of apples, or pickles will add some crunch to your sandwich. Which do you like best?

George Washington Carver was an American scientist.

Food

Peanuts are close relatives of peas. Although they were first grown in South America, peanuts found an important home in the United States. George Washington Carver found more than 300 different ways to use peanuts. Your favorite use for peanuts is probably peanut butter. Ask an adult to help you make the recipe above.

11

The Constitution explains how the government will work.

This is the most famous picture of George Washington, first president of the United States. It was painted by Gilbert Stuart in 1796.

Government

The Constitution says that the country shall have a President, a Congress, and a Supreme Court. It explains how those leaders will be chosen. It also explains how the government of each state will work together with the federal government. The Constitution also explains the individual rights enjoyed by every U.S. citizen.

By voting, Americans decide who their president will be and who will represent them in Congress. Voters in the United States are the most important parts of their government.

History

John Adams, Thomas Jefferson, and Benjamin Franklin are among the men at the desk to sign the Declaration of Independence in this famous painting.

The United States used to be ruled by England. In 1776, a group of Americans met in Philadelphia. They were about to tell the king of England that they were no longer going to obey him. The king had already sent a large army to force the Americans to obey his laws. The Americans thought these laws were unfair. The men decided to write down all of the reasons they were angry with the king. This **document** came to be known as the Declaration of Independence. John Hancock was the first to sign the document on July 4, 1776.

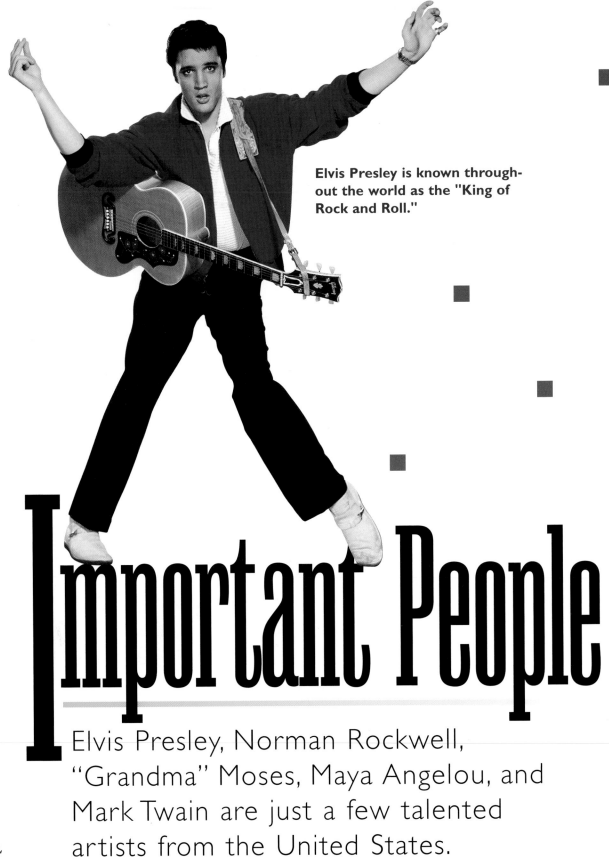

Elvis Presley is known through-
out the world as the "King of
Rock and Roll."

Important People

Elvis Presley, Norman Rockwell,
"Grandma" Moses, Maya Angelou, and
Mark Twain are just a few talented
artists from the United States.

Grandma Moses was 70 years old when she began her career as a painter.

Norman Rockwell paints an American scene in his New York studio in 1933.

Maya Angelou is an award-winning writer and actress.

Norman Rockwell painted pictures about life in the United States. They reminded people that it was good to live in America. Sometimes, his pictures were funny. His most famous paintings appeared on the covers of magazines.

Grandma Moses lived to be 101 years old. Her simple paintings of country scenes are now found in museums. She showed Americans that it is never too late to follow their dreams.

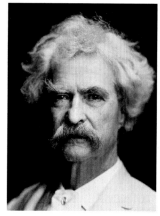

Mark Twain wrote many books that described life in America along the Mississippi River.

The work of a coal miner is dangerous and dirty.

Many jobs in the United States require skills with technology, such as manufacturing computer chips.

Jobs

Many people in the United States have jobs that make use of the country's rich **natural resources**. They use wood to build homes. They use iron to manufacture cars and machinery. They mine coal and gas to provide power for factories.

Other Americans, such as teachers or bankers, have jobs that serve others. In some ways, the United States measures its success by the number of people who have jobs.

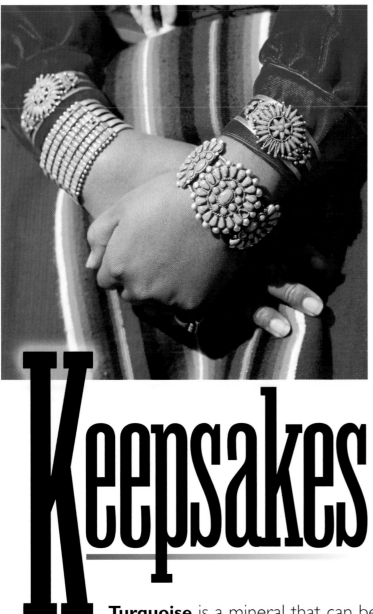

Some of the most skilled makers of turquoise jewelry are the Native American peoples in the Southwest.

A Hawaiian girl performs a traditional dance of welcome while wearing leis.

Keepsakes

Turquoise is a mineral that can be found in certain kinds of rocks in Arizona and New Mexico. It is a beautiful blue-green color. Have you ever bought something made of turquoise? Turquoise is usually combined with silver to create bracelets, rings, and necklaces.

Have you ever worn a necklace made of flowers? **Leis** are made with flowers. They can be found in Hawaii. Leis are worn for special occasions, either around the neck or as a headband. Sometimes, they are made with shells and feathers.

17

Land

All kinds of landscapes can be found in the United States.

Many famous Western movies were filmed at beautiful Monument Valley in Arizona.

On the country's coasts you will find rocky coastlines and sandy beaches. In the Southwest you will see deserts. In the Southeast, wetlands, such as the Florida Everglades, are common. Much of the middle of the United States is covered by a huge **prairie**. Mountain ranges run the length of the country in the East and the West.

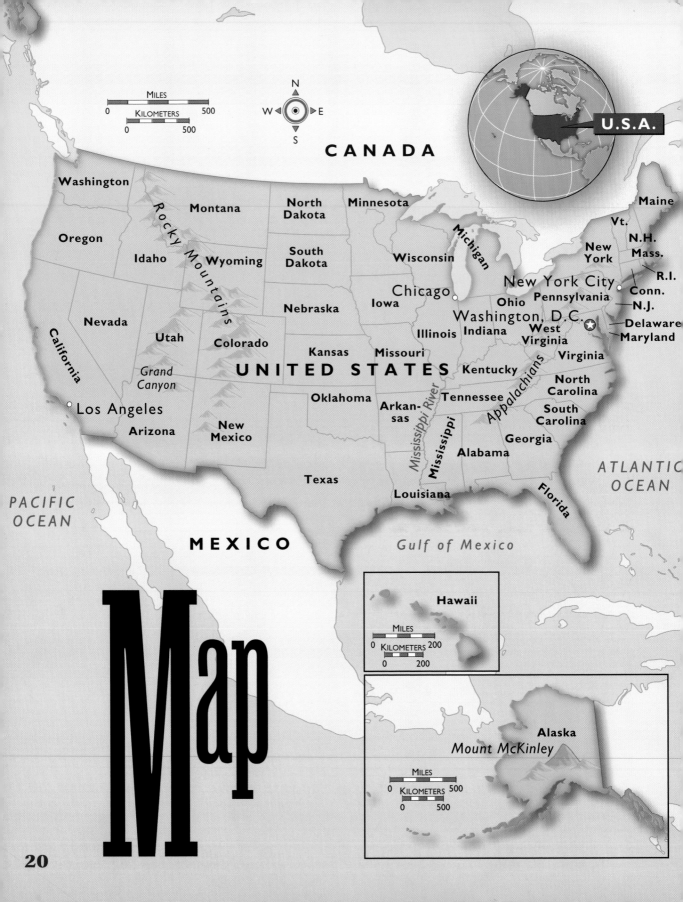

MILES
0 _____ 500
KILOMETERS
0 _____ 500

N
W ◄ ◆ ► E
S

U.S.A.

CANADA

Washington

Montana

North Dakota

Minnesota

Maine

Oregon

Idaho

Wyoming

South Dakota

Wisconsin

Michigan

Vt.

N.H.

New York

Mass.

R.I.

New York City

Conn.

N.J.

Nevada

Utah

Colorado

Nebraska

Iowa

Chicago

Ohio

Pennsylvania

Rocky Mountains

California

Grand Canyon

Kansas

Missouri

Illinois

Indiana

Washington, D.C.

West Virginia

Delaware

Maryland

Virginia

Los Angeles

Arizona

New Mexico

Oklahoma

Arkan- sas

UNITED STATES

Kentucky

Tennessee

Appalachians

North Carolina

South Carolina

Texas

Mississippi River

Mississippi

Alabama

Georgia

ATLANTIC OCEAN

Louisiana

Florida

PACIFIC OCEAN

MEXICO

Gulf of Mexico

Map

Hawaii

MILES
0 _____ 200
KILOMETERS
0 _____ 200

Alaska

Mount McKinley

MILES
0 _____ 500
KILOMETERS
0 _____ 500

20

Nation

You probably know that the thirteen red-and-white stripes on the nation's flag are symbols for the thirteen original colonies. But did you know that the top and bottom stripes must always be red ones? This makes the flag easier to see from a long distance. A star is added to the flag whenever a state becomes part of the country. The last time a star was added was in 1959. That was the year Hawaii became the fiftieth state.

Covered wagons carried many families onto the frontier.

Only in USA

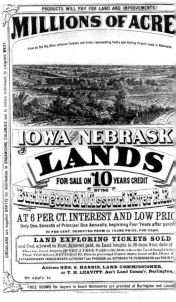

Posters like this one encouraged farmers to buy land in the midwestern states.

Frontier is a word that means "beyond what is known." Much of the history of the United States has been about people moving into new frontiers.

The Transcontinental Railroad was finished with the driving of the Golden Spike in Promontory, Utah, on May 10, 1869. The railroad made it easier for people to travel from coast to coast.

Settlers race to claim the best plots of land during the Oklahoma Land Rush of 1893.

In the United States, the frontier has been in different places at different times. Usually, the frontier was a place to the west of where most people lived. This was because the first thirteen colonies were on the East Coast. The government often made it easy for people to own land on the frontier. Land was given away or offered to people for very little money. Movement into these areas almost always meant that Native Americans lost their land.

People

The United States is home to people of many different skin colors and ancestry.

Inuit boy

The United States is a country of **immigrants**. For hundreds of years, people have traveled from far away to live in the United States.

An African American father plays with his two daughters.

Sometimes, the Unites States is called a "melting pot." This means that people from many different nations have come together to become a completely new nation. The United States is special because it is made up of people from so many different places. In the United States, people enjoy being "American," but they also like to remember the places where their ancestors lived. Today, all but about eight percent of Americans were born in the United States.

This Chinese American fisherman was photographed in San Francisco, which is home to a large Chinese American population.

QUESTION

Where Is the Curviest Street In the World?

The answer is San Francisco, California! Lombard Street is one of the city's top tourist attractions. It is very steep, and driving down it can be tricky. It has eight sharp curves from top to bottom. It is also very narrow. Cars are not allowed to drive from the bottom of the hill to the top. Lombard Street was never really meant to be used by cars. Its curves were built to help horses and wagons go up the hill.

San Francisco is famous for its hilly, curved streets. This is Lombard Street, the curviest street in the world.

It took 83 years, from 1907 to 1990, to build the National Cathedral in Washington, D.C.

Religion

Americans have many different kinds of freedom. One of the most important to them is the freedom of religion. Freedom of religion means that they can make their own choices about how they worship. The government cannot force them to practice any particular religion.

The majority of Americans are Christian. They belong to Roman Catholic, Baptist, Lutheran, and many other Christian churches. Other religions, such as Judaism, Islam, and Buddhism, have fewer members. No matter how few, the Constitution protects their right to worship freely.

School & Sports

Most children in the United States attend public schools. Public schools are found in neighborhoods. The taxes collected from people who live there help to pay for the things needed by each school. A smaller number of students attend private or religious schools.

American football is played by many professional and school teams. Baseball, soccer, and basketball are other popular team sports played in the United States.

Professional football is one of the most popular spectator sports in the United States.

Commuters, like these in New Jersey, fill the highways during rush hours.

Transportation

Once, automobiles were built very slowly. Workers built one car before starting another. Cars were expensive, and few people could afford one. Henry Ford was a man who had a better idea. He made it possible for factories to build many cars at the same time. More Americans could afford to buy one of Ford's cars. Owning a car meant that they could go places and do things they had never been able to do. Cars changed America forever. In the United States today, there are 75 cars for every 100 people.

Henry Ford's "Model T" was the first car owned by many Americans.

The faces of preside (from left to right) George Washington Thomas Jefferson, Theodore Roosevel and Abraham Linco can be seen at Mou Rushmore.

Unusual Places

Mount Rushmore is near Rapid City, South Dakota. It is an important symbol of the United States and one of the country's most-visited **monuments**. Gutzon Borglum was the man who had the idea for carving faces of the four presidents into the mountain.

It took more than fourteen years to complete his sculpture. Borglum did not live to see his project finished. Following his death, the work was taken over by his son Lincoln. The faces of the presidents are as tall as five-story buildings!

Part of the Smithsonian Institution, the Air and Space Museum, contains many actual vehicles from the history of flight.

Visiting the Country

People have a nickname for the Smithsonian Institution. They call it "the nation's attic." This is because lots of things from the past are stored there. The Smithsonian's collection includes objects from television shows and movies. It includes portraits of the presidents, and gowns worn by the first ladies. At the Smithsonian, you can see everything from moon rocks to gigantic airplanes. The Smithsonian is actually several different museums in Washington, D.C. Plan on staying a long time when you visit the nation's attic!

Martin Luther King, Jr.

Window to the Past

One hundred years after the end of slavery, life in the United States was still hard for many African Americans. In some places, they had to obey different laws than their white neighbors.

People from many places came to the March on Washington to demonstrate for freedom and civil rights.

Rosa Parks is famous because she stopped obeying an unfair law.

These laws kept them from being completely free. They could not go places or do the things that other Americans could. Many people felt these laws were wrong. They began to stop obeying them. Large groups of people began to march together. Lawmakers began to see how many people wanted the laws to be changed. The biggest of these marches was the March on Washington in 1963. Martin Luther King, Jr., gave a famous speech to the crowd. He told them that he dreamed of the time when all Americans would be treated with the same kind of fairness.

Thurgood Marshall was the first African American to become a U.S. Supreme Court Justice.

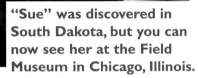

"Sue" was discovered in South Dakota, but you can now see her at the Field Museum in Chicago, Illinois.

X-tra Special Things

The Statue of Liberty is a symbol of freedom to many Americans.

One of Kilauea's many craters erupted in 1984.

These rock drawings were made by people who lived near Dinosaur National Monument more than 1,000 years ago.

The huge giant sequoia tree grows from a seed the size of a grain of wheat.

There are many special things in the United States. "Sue" is the largest fossil of a tyrannosaurus rex that has ever been found. Sue is named after the person who discovered her, Susan Hendrickson. In Colorado, Dinosaur National Monument is home to other amazing discoveries. There, visitors can see the fossils of many different kinds of **prehistoric** animals.

Kilauea is a volcano on the island of Hawaii. It is one of the world's most active volcanoes. It has been erupting for hundreds of years.

California's giant sequoia trees are some of the oldest and largest living things on the planet. The biggest of them is the General Sherman Tree. It is 274-feet (84-m) tall and more than 2,000-years old!

Colorful floats and costumes are a popular part of Mardi Gras, a popular celebration each year in New Orleans, Louisiana. In other parts of the world it is known as Carnival.

Yearly Festivals

Americans celebrate many of the same holidays that are celebrated in other parts of the world.

Thanksgiving meals remind Americans of the many things for which they can be thankful.

Veterans salute the flag during a Memorial Day parade.

"Uncle Sam" pedals down Main Street in a Fourth-of-July parade.

Some holidays, though, are special only to the United States. One such holiday is Memorial Day. It began as a day to remember soldiers who died during the Civil War. Now, it honors men and women who gave their lives in all American wars. On Memorial Day, graves are decorated with flags and flowers.

Another special holiday is Thanksgiving. It is a day when Americans remember the beginnings of their nation. They think about the courage of the Pilgrims. They remember the kindness shown by the Native Americans. They say "thank-you" for being able to live in the United States.

Zydeco musicians perform as part of a Mardi Gras celebration in Louisiana.

Zydeco

Zydeco is a rollicking kind of music that comes from Louisiana. In zydeco, the melody is played on an accordion. Other instruments provide a rhythmic background. It is difficult to listen to zydeco and not feel happy. Zydeco is just one of many kinds of music that developed in the United States.

Country music, the blues, rock-and-roll, jazz, and hip-hop are all musical styles that first became popular in America.

■ English Words

bison (BYE-suhn) a large, grass-eating mammal, also known as the buffalo

borough (BUR-oh) a smaller part of a large city, often having its own government

document (DOK-yuh-muhnt) a piece of paper with important information on it

frontier (fruhn-TIHR) "beyond what is known," the edge of a country where few people travel

immigrant (IM-uh-nuhnt) one who moves to a new country

industry (IN-duh-stree) a group of people that make and sell a product or service

landmark (LAND-mark) a building or scenic object that is associated with the place around it

leis (LAYZ) wreaths of flowers or other materials worn for special occasions in Hawaii

monument (MON-yuh-muhnt) an area or object that is set aside and protected because of its beauty or importance

natural resources (NACH-ur-uhl REE-sorss) materials that appear in nature—such as water, trees, and soil—that can be used to manufacture other things

prairie (PRAIR-ee) a type of mostly flat land, usually covered with grass

prehistoric (pree-hi-STOR-ik) before history; usually, long before humans appeared on earth

site a place of interest to historians or scientists

turquoise (TUR-kwoiz) a type of blue-green mineral

zydeco a style of music from Louisiana

■ Let's Explore More

Look What Came from the United States by Kevin Davis, Franklin Watts, 1999

Red, White, Blue, and Uncle Who? The Stories behind Some of America's Patriotic Symbols by Teresa Bateman, Holiday House, 2001

The United States of America by Christine and David Petersen, Children's Press, 1999

Websites

http://smithsonianeducation.org
The Smithsonian Institution sponsors this website that describes its museums, and allows you to go behind the scenes to see parts of its collection that even visitors to the museums can't see!

http://www.americasstory.com
Read about amazing Americans, play games, and listen to music on this website sponsored by the Library of Congress.

 Index

Italic page numbers indicate illustrations.

Meet the Author

JEFF REYNOLDS was raised on a farm in Illinois. He has lived in Minneapolis-St. Paul, New York City, and Connecticut, and now lives and works in Washington, D.C. He received a B.A. from Western Illinois University and an M.A. in Theater History and Criticism from Brooklyn College. At various times he has been a farmer, milk man, school custodian, housepainter, hotel bellman, stamp dealer, teacher, librarian, actor, journalist, and editor. He is also the author of *A to Z books* about Germany, Japan, Puerto Rico, and United States of America.